Ghost o

Charles Robertson

Published by

Bottle Tree Productions

DEDICATION

Dedicated to Macaroni and Hannibal for breathing such
wonderful life into the play.

Cover photo by David Ajax

CONTENTS

Notes about the Play

The female characters are all given the generic name of *Girl*. This is because The Girl is both actor and character. Part of the richness of theatre is the initial separation and subsequent joining of actor and character. We, as audience members, are fascinated by the magic and ritual of theatre. In this play, the audience gets to watch the machinery of theatre at work. In between scenes, The Ghost is the dresser and The Girl is the actor During the scenes, The Ghost becomes the feminine essence, and The Girl alternatively becomes a homeless girl, a cocaine addict, a hippie, a fifties housewife, a lesbian artist, a brain-damaged girl and a young English bride. In this way, the play incorporates the ritual and magic of theatre with the play's emotional realism.

Original music from a live musician would add a lot to the emotional tone of the play. A musician can add ambience, emotion and sound effects. A musician can also set up a scene with appropriate music indicative of the time. A musician on stage shows simultaneously the artist and his work, without taking away from the play. Otherwise, recorded music can be used. Original music enhances. Well-known music takes away.

Lighting should be simple. A leaf gobbo to suggest the sunlight or moonlight coming through the leaves onto the stage would be a simple way of representing the tree. A gobbo is a metal cut-out that fits into certain stage lights. The shape of the cut-out is seen as a larger and similarly shaped shadow on the stage. Therefore, the young woman on stage will seem to be underneath the tree. There should be a circle of light; centre stage, from which the character of The Girl cannot exit. Outside the circle would be the tree and the musician if there is one. The Ghost can be outside this circle when she does not have lines or actions to interact with the young woman. If The Ghost is outside the circle of light she must always focus her attention on the young woman. The lights on the tree, and the musician should be dimmer, so that the audience's attention is always focused on the young woman.

The set can be very simple with a stool placed centre stage, for the young woman, a simple representation of a tree on stage right. and a stool or chair, placed stage left for the musician, if one is being used.

ACKNOWLEDGMENTS

Special Thanks to Michael Catlin for agreeing to helm the original production of the play. His sensitive and creative direction added so much to the finished product.

And to my business partner; Anne Marie; for all her work and support.

ACT ONE

SCENE 1 The Homeless Girl

DOWNSTAGE RIGHT

Under a dark blue light is a representation of a tree. Draped on the branches are assorted pieces of costume and accessories-all of them totally red, or with red as a dominant colour except for a glass and a long cigarette holder which can sit on the floor in front of the tree.

DOWNSTAGE CENTRE

is a stool-in front of which lies a red jacket. Lit by Leaf gobbo.

DOWNSTAGE LEFT

is a chair or stool for a musician if one is going to be used.

Charles Robertson

Lights Fade.

Stage in Darkness.

Ghost of the Tree is essentially eight monologues, and works best in a minimalist setting since the words convey the images. The first monologue and the last one are by the same character. There are seven different characters plus the ghost. The seven characters can be played by one actor or up to seven different actors. The play is about the dissolution of a family tree and the part each ghost has played in this inevitable decline. The tree is a metaphor for their corrupted family line.

The stage directions and music suggestions are only that. The costumes pieces and props have red in them because they suggest the blood of the family line. My suggestion would be that the scene changes and character changes are obvious so that the audience is as entertained by the work of the actor as they are by the story. The transition from one character to another can almost be ritualistic. Each prop or costume item is invested with power. When the actor gives up a costume piece or prop, she gives up the character and becomes neutral. When she accepts a new costume or prop she accepts the new character. Instead of speeding through the character changes,

2

the actors should be slow and deliberate. There should be lighting and music specific to the scene changes. These transitions and scene changes should be as compelling as the show itself. In that way, an audience does not lose its focus, does not come out of the play.

In the darkness a woman can be heard singing Mockingbird.

Lights slowly up on two figures-One is the woman who is singing. She is sitting on the floor. She represents the Ghost of the Tree. She is the feminine essence of the different generations of women in this particular family tree. She will be a spiritual guide for the Girl and the other characters in the story, leading the audience on a journey of discovery into this family's past. The ghost will also occasionally act as chorus, and as intermittent characters in the story. She will also act as a dresser for the actor during the transitions between scenes. The ghost will never leave the stage, only moving out of and into the light. But she will always be watching-focusing her energy on the living girl. The ghost can wear whatever she wants, but she must be ethereal.

Lying on her lap is a girl, approximately 18-22 years of age. She is dressed in black except for the red coat that was lying on the stage in preset. Her acting area is restricted to the centre-stage area. The tree is off-limits. The idea for staging is that the girl is confined to the the light that illuminates centre stage. The ghost is not so limited. She can go into the centre stage light to be with the girl, or out of the light in the shadows or at the tree. In this way, it is suggested that the ghost can travel between life and death, between shadow and light.

Melancholic Music.

GIRL: *(Sitting up as if waking from a dream)*

Mom…I thought…

GHOST: *(Stands up. She is spiritual-ethereal)*

The house is empty now. Empty of all life. But outside in the darkness in that tree planted too close to the house, the shadows wait, the shadows wait for a soul to join them.

(There is now a larger pool of light and the leaf gobbo is still evident. The light should suggest evening)

(The ghost moves back out of the light and watches from the shadows)

Ghost of the Tree

(Music fades)

GIRL: Mom! Mom! Where are you? I came home.
I'm back. See. Here I am. Mom? The England House.
Why do they call it that? Mom; why do they call it
that? England house. Things'll be different. You'll
see. Remember when I was little, I loved this room.
At night the stars would stretch up like a ladder into
heaven. And when it rained, it was the comfortabelest
feeling in the world. On top of the world. Look. See
that tree there. See it. It's dead now. The branches are
always scratching at the window. When there's a
storm, you can hear them rubbing against the house,
against the glass. Like monsters trying to get in.
When I was little, those branches, and its noises, used
to scare the crap out of me, but some of the branches
came down in a storm. After a while everything dies,
even a big monster tree.

GHOST: *(Walking around the circle of light)*

After a while everything dies, even a big monster
tree. After a while everything dies, even a big
monster tree.

GIRL: *(Speaking at the same time)*

I remember there being light here. It's cold now. It's getting dark. People talking in my head, in my brain. Talking.

GHOST: Talking, talking...talk.

GIRL: *(Sits at the stool as if it is a kitchen table)*

I remember sitting in my jammies at the kitchen table. Mom; remember me sitting at the kitchen table with my knees pulled up to my chin, eating cereal. Cold cereal and milk. A kid without a care in the world.

(Confiding in the audience)

My mom; she had these dreams for me. Wanted me to be a movie star. Had these, uh, professional pictures done of me. Got me into acting classes. Got me an agent. He was a scam guy, but I guess that didn't really matter, cause, well the problem was, I had no talent, no real talent. I couldn't act, or maybe I could but the noise in my head, the voices in my head...

One day my mom dropped me off here, at my gramma, granddads. Said she'd be right back. I waited on the front step. I waited and waited...but she never came back.

(Approaches audience)

Grammy took care of me. She was an angel, one of those angels that light up the night. She used to write children's stories about Africa. Told me I could be whatever I wanted to be, that I could go to Africa and help the poor.

Help the poor?

Who's going to help me? Who's going to take care of me?

Wish I was little. Wish I could start over.

When my grammy got sick, everything turned to crap. My granddad; he couldn't handle me, couldn't take care of me. He tried to get a hold of my mom, but I dunno, she was gone. So I got farmed out, farmed out to foster care. My life keeps sliding away from me.

(Pulling coat tightly around herself)

And then at fourteen I was on the streets, doing whatever to survive, but being on the streets was better than all the homes I was stuck in, cause in those places, those homes, they never accepted me. They had all these rules for me, like I was some sort of animal, some sort of dog. No love left over for me.

Charles Robertson

Nobody wanted me. They just wanted their monthly cheque from the government. I was a cheque, a number, an inconvenience.

(Noticing the emptiness of the stage)

I came home. I came home tonight. I came here, because I had nowhere else to go. I thought I could talk to my granddad, ask him for help, but there's nobody here. It's like a grave. A goddamn grave.

(To audience)

I been on the street for four years now. It's bad out there. You gotta know how to handle yourself. You gotta be tough cause there's a lot of screwed-up people out there.

Like I can't get welfare 'cause I don't got no permanent address. Like you need a home to get money from the government, and the shelters, the shelters are more dangerous than the streets.

Like sometimes I can con my way into a friend's home for a while. Get cleaned up. But that's only for a while.

(She poses)

I wonder what kinda actress I coulda been.

Ghost of the Tree

(To the audience)

Like, it's like a fork in the road, where you make a decision, but sometimes there is no decision because of the kind of person you are. Like maybe, like they say, everybody has free will, but I don't think so, I think you do what you do because you're programmed that way. Not like programmed at birth and shit, that's gotta be part of it, but I mean the words in your head, all the stuff that happens to you, stays in you.

And words like no, and you can't do that, and whore. And words like I'll give you twenty bucks if you...

GHOST: *(Speaking at the same time as above)*

Where's Johnny? Get out of the store! Bitch! Let me go!

GIRL: Words that mess you up and stop you from getting out of the shit hole that you're in...

I spent a weekend at some rich guy's house. He was like a judge or something. It was real nice. There was like two forks at dinner. Class. A whirlpool. An elevator in the house. A friggin' elevator in the house...

The next night, I'm eating a slice of pizza I found in a garbage can…It was still warm.

(Getting up on top of stool)

Best place to sleep is on a rooftop. 'Cause there's like these, I dunno, hot air vents, and you're pretty safe up there if you find a special place, but I don't like sleeping down on the street.

(Gets off the stool and moves downstage)

There's this old guy I know. Crazy guy; Hank. He used to talk to me. Used to talk to me about how the bible, was some sort of proof of alien visitations to earth. Anyway, what was I talking about?...Yeah. Hank. He was sleeping in some public washroom and these guys came in and pissed all over him. So he smelled like piss all the time. I can't take it, being out there…

(Melancholic music starts again)

(To her imagined mother)

Mom, I'm getting married. We're gonna fix up this place, fix it up like it used to be. Johnny; he's got some plans. Johnny's great. I love him mom. Only something happened. Something's happening to me.

Mom. I got a baby comin', and I need some help. I never had no baby before. And something's not right. And like there's this blood. And…

(Fighting back her tears)

Some paint and nails, we can fix up the place. But the baby. I could sure use some advice. Some help.

(Despairing)

Mom, I did something bad. I tried to…I did something real bad.

SCENE 2   The Cocaine Addict

Transition Scene.

Muted Eighties music as if from another room.

The Girl sits motionless on the stool.

There is an overhead light and leaf gobbo.

The Ghost takes off the girl's coat and hangs it on one of the branches of the tree.

The Ghost grabs some red beads from the tree and places them around the girl's neck and then she puts the girl's hair up. The Ghost moves downstage.

End of Transition.

Lights up-leaf gobbo gone.

GIRL: (*Getting up*)

I'm pumped. I'm really pumped.

(Bumps into the Ghost)

Don't shove. This guy just gave this to me.

(Shows off an imaginary bag of cocaine)

Nice eh? Place on the waterfront sold. I got two other fish on the hook. Yeah, things are going great. I'm going places. Its like everyone else is trudging along in slow motion and I'm just passing them right by.

GHOST: (*Starts applying lipstick in front of an imaginary mirror downstage centre*)

GIRL: (*Sits on stool with her back to the audience- Music slows as she does a line of coke*)

(*When she stands up music picks up tempo*)

This stuff is great! Makes your mind as sharp as a tack, as sharp as a goddamn tack!

THE GHOST: (*Has an imaginary party of friends with her and is clearly annoyed with the Girl who continually tries to get her attention*)

GIRL: Ya gotta be aggressive. Can't take no for an answer. Just beat the shit out of the client til he can't take it no more. I don't care what the price is long as I sell. Selling is the greatest high in the world.

I sold a condemned building to a senior looking for a place to retire. Really scratched her eyes out on that one.

See that big old world out there. Ninety nine percent of them are nothing. They're sheep. They exist for us. The smart. The go-getters.

Oh! My nose is bleeding! Do you have a Kleenex or something? Toilet paper?

GHOST: (*Retrieves mimed toilet paper*)

GIRL: Come on! Hurry up! I don't wanna get nothing on this dress. The thing is...

(Sticking toilet paper in her nose. Music slows down)

The thing is…

(Music speeds up)

Men are weak. Men are like guppies waiting to be scooped up and put in a pail. Ya gotta put your morals in a pail. The thing is,

(She slows down)

I love this music.

(To Ghost)

Guess what my name is? You'll never guess. To look at me you wouldn't think... Rainbow. My name is Rainbow. Yeah, what's yours? No, really. My mom was a hippie. She thought I'd have; I don't know. What's a rainbow like? Guess it's about the pot at the end of the rainbow. Rainy for short, which I guess is just opposite to what its supposed to mean.

(Music slows down)

Thing is...Think I'm losing my memory. Thing is. What was I saying?

(Music speeds up)

(To Ghost)

You're really great you know. I love the things you say. You're like an incredible talker.

(To Mirror)

Incredible talker. Do I look hot or what? You are so great. No, not me. Yes you. You're great! You're so goddamn gorgeous! Wait! Wait! I know what you're going to say. You're going to say that I'm just saying that. You're going to say, what was I saying? You're going to say. Oh yeah...You're going to say that I'm just blowing smoke.

(Slows down)

Hot air.

Charles Robertson

(To Ghost-up tempo)

Hot air ballooning. Ever been? I wanna go. Why don't we rent ourselves a hot air balloon later this morning and watch the sun come up, watch it hanging like a big bubble in the sky, waiting for the morning to explode.

Who's with you? Don't tell me it's that hunk, that guy. You watch it honey, I'll steal him from you.

(Girl grabs lipstick from Ghost and applies it)

I will take him from right under your nose. 'Cause I got the look, plus I'm stinking rich.

(Hands lipstick back and continues talking to Ghost)

Do you wanna know how rich? Do you wanna know how rich I am? Do you? I don't know. I'm so rich, I don't know.

(To mirror-speeding up tempo)

Money is just a number. That's the secret. Money is just a number and you try to get as many of those little numbers as you can. I just borrow. Just keep maxing out my credit and then they give me more credit.

I got a big old house, well it's my parents. The England House. Architectural masterpiece. Got a second mortgage on it. Almost lost the whole thing when that tree beside it got hit by lightning. Boom! Knocked me out of my bed, like being touched by God, or burned alive by God, or something by God. And then another one, another house…and then…I have a jag.

(To Ghost)

I have investments, see. Investments are a steal. Sometimes you lose, but it's like Darwin said, survival of the fittest.

(Physically aggressive)

Kick the shit out of the other animals. You know, if I lived in the forest I would be a lion, a goddamn, freakin', massive lion.

(She growls)

There's a guy out there I want, and I'm gonna get him too, 'cause there's no other alternative. Its destiny. Instinct. See I want it, and I get it, 'cause I don't have anything holding me back; no scruples. I will do whatever, whenever. I deserve it all. You gotta think that way. Positive thinking and a lot of this shit and you can fly. The world is your oyster…

(Music stops)

GHOST: (*To imaginary friends*)

Look at her. She's pregnant!

GIRL: What? Yeah. So what? So freakin' what? I'm having a baby. I dunno. Could be anybody's, but I'll find some poor sap, or I'll kill it. Oh yeah, I could do that. It would only get in my way.

(Ghost exits)

This is the eighties, and the individual is king. And I am the king king. And this is my castle.

(Lights down to a spot)

(Girl sinks to the floor overcome by fear)

I…uh…What's happening? Something's happening to me. Someone? Anyone? Where is everybody?...What?…Excuse me...Can I get out of here, Doctor? I gotta go home. I'm all right. I'm all… right. No...No. Just a little champagne. Excuse me? I'm pregnant. I know. I sell real estate. If you're in the market. It's dog eat dog and I'm gonna be top dog!…Top dog.

Excuse me. Am I dying?

How's my baby? Is she okay?

I'm really cold you know and...and I feel all sweaty.

You ever had a cat? Doctor? Oh all right. Nurse. You ever had a cat? I remember it used to curl up at night near my head and I could hear it purring, but it scared me; the cat. At night when it looked at me, it's eyes would glow. Like demon's eyes. Am I gonna die?

Yeah, I want this kid. I really do. Do you think you could take it out now? Please. It hurts. Could you take it out? Please, someone…?

(Clutches at her beads)

No, don't touch that.

(Like a frightened child)

It was my mom's. And she loved me. My mom loved me.

SCENE 3   The Hippie Girl

Transition Scene.

Sixties folk music.

The Girl sits motionless on the stool.

There is an overhead light and leaf gobbo.

The Ghost removes the necklace from the Girl and returns it to the tree. The Ghost takes a poncho from the tree and puts it on the girl. She undoes the girl's hair and lets it hang loose.

End of Transition.

The Girl gets off the stool and sits on the floor in front of the stool.

The Ghost sits down beside her.

The light should suggest this scene takes place outside in day-time. Add the leaf gobbo to suggest the girl is sitting in the shade.

GIRL: Here I sit in my backyard, in the shade of my tree, my big old oak tree.

(The Ghost is smoking an imaginary joint; a marijuana cigarette)

Ghost of the Tree

(If there is a musician, he or she could sit on the stool and play music, as if he or she is a character in the scene, a hippie musician friend of the Girl and the Ghost)

GIRL: Here I write stories, stories about animals, about places, about places I have never been, about dreams, about this tree.

(The Ghost passes the joint to the Girl-The Girl's lines will have to be broken up by the act of her smoking-such as inhaling and perhaps coughing. She will pass it back and forth between her and the Ghost and perhaps the musician. She can be holding it between her fingers for a while as she contemplates the deep thoughts she is having. The handling of the joint should be slow and low-key)

We have this big hole in my back yard. I don't know why. I don't know why it's here. I get stoned sometimes and sit in the hole, hide in the hole,

(To tree as Music fades)

and watch the children playing in my tree fort. I love children. They are so innocent. They have the whole world ahead of them. I am going to have a hundred of them, a hundred children just like that big oak,

(To the audience)

hundreds of little saplings that will grow up strong and pure with respect for all races, all people, and I pray my child is stronger than me. Perhaps she can go to Africa instead of just dreaming about it, or maybe to South America as a missionary to help those less fortunate. I will call my child...

(At this point the Girl can inhale the smoke from the joint, and then slowly let it out before saying Rainbow)

Rainbow, because I think the rainbow is the most beautiful of God's gifts, like angels lighting up the sky after a storm, and it shows how different colours can live together, in harmony, in peace.

Like there's this guy, Desmond.

(Looks at the Ghost and the Musician and smiles. The Girl then turns to the audience)

We're really into each other. We're gonna go down to Africa and help the starving, the poor people of the earth. I mean, we have so much and they have so little. Save the wildlife too, 'cause lions and elephants and hippos; they're vanishing and I want to do something about it.

I know I have something important to say because I believe in stuff, like women's rights and gay rights, animals, the Vietnamese. Everybody. I believe in everybody. And I'm against stuff, too, like the war. Like killing is wrong.

(She puts out the joint. The following change in tone would suggest that she has been self-medicating-The drugs are used to help her escape from reality)

GHOST and MUSICIAN: *(Get up to leave)*

GIRL: *(Hugs Ghost. When she turns to the musician, he or she is gone-She turns to the audience)*

My mom tried to kill herself. She did. And now her brain is fried…empty. Nobody home...and I don't want to talk about her.

My dad...I don't want to talk about him either- My dad has a girlfriend. She's his secretary, and I hate her with all my heart. And she stays in our house! How could he do that to my mom? What's wrong with him?

(Looks up at the tree)

When I was little, me and my brother built this tree fort beside the house, and it would be our safe place, our castle in the sky...and we could see into the back bedroom, see my mom sitting there like a zombie, staring out the window. Staring at nothing,

(To the audience)

or maybe she's like God, and can see everything, see what a mess I'm making of my life.

I cried when my cat Sparkles died. I don't cry about my mom. I can't cry about my mom. She never got to do anything with her life.

My mom thought I would be the perfect little suburban angel, the light in the dark world. But I'm not. I'm nothing.

(She sits on the stool-Music starts up again)

Here I sit in this big hole in the backyard. Hide in the hole...get stoned.

(She gets up and takes an imaginary photo out of her pocket and shows audience-Music stops)

Here's a picture of my mom. It's my favourite. This picture I like because she's laughing.

I never saw my mom laugh before.

SCENE 4 *The Fifties Housewife*

Transition Scene.

Music suggesting the fifties.

The Girl sits motionless on the stool.

There is an overhead light and leaf gobbo.

The Ghost takes off the Girl's poncho and hangs it up on one of the branches of the tree. The Ghost takes a red apron from the tree and approaches the Girl. The Girl stands up and the Ghost ties the apron around the girl's waist. The Ghost then puts the Girl's hair up. The Ghost remains close to the Girl.

End of Transition.

The Sound of a Ticking Clock.

Lights up full.

GHOST: You are a picture of happiness, cleanliness and order. You love your home.

(The Ghost walks out of the light-The Music stops)

Tick tock...Tick tock...Tick tock

GIRL: (*To the audience*)

The clock is ticking the seconds of my life away. The tap drips but will not stop. I can't get it to stop. I have cleaned the upstairs thirty-one seconds faster than I did yesterday.

(*The Sound of the Clock fades out*)

It's such a huge house. It's too big really.

We rent the upstairs rooms to students.

My husband sells insurance. People need insurance so that when something bad happens they can get covered, covered with money. My husband dreams of fires, floods and theft. In the morning when the alarm goes off,

(*Mimes pouring coffee*)

I get up and I put on the coffee. He needs his coffee. It makes him feel alive.

(*Touches her tummy*)

I am pregnant. I am hoping for a boy. Boys have a future.

(*Mimes cleaning*)

Ghost of the Tree

I am proud of my house cleaning. I shine the counters
and the floors, so that I can see my reflection. I clean
the mirrors so that they shine. I clean out the
wastepaper baskets,

(Cleans behind the stool)

and behind the toilet where the grunge gets.

(To the audience slightly disturbed)

There is a scratch on the linoleum. I don't know how
it got there but it distresses me, because dirt builds up
in there. I can't get it out. I phoned my mother but she
doesn't seem to care. She only talks about how
unhappy she is with Harry.

*(Ghost mimes advertising a cleaning product with a
big smile on her face).*

I watch the commercials on t.v. for the best cleaning
products, but no matter what I buy, the dirt just will
not come out.

(Ghost exits the light)

My husband wants to build a bomb shelter in the back
yard.

(Girl looks at aborted bomb shelter)

Well, he started it. Last summer, he dug a hole. The hole is still there. I think it makes our yard look ugly. Weeds grow in the hole,

(The Ghost becomes a bitter-looking Mrs. Harbour)

(The Girl gets down on her knees)

and I have to get down on my hands and knees in the dirt and pick those weeds. I can see old Mrs Harbour watching me from her bedroom window.

(Girl and Ghost wave at each other)

She does nothing but watch me from her window…I think she's a witch.

(Girl gets up and goes to the back of the stool and mimes picking plastic flowers out of a vase)

I have plastic flowers in my house. They are the latest thing and they will never die. I just have to wash them in the sink with the dripping tap, and they are as good as new.

(Moves forward to audience)

I am afraid of having my baby. My mother tells me horrible stories and she says that she wishes that I was never born, that I remind her of the asshole that got her pregnant.

My husband leaves for work at eight-thirty on the dot, eight-thirty on the nose. And he comes back like clockwork at 4, or 5, or 6, or sometimes he doesn't come home at all.

(Stands straight up, hands at her sides, as if she is lying on a bed)

I lie in bed and look at the ceiling until he comes home. I have made up lists, lists of chores, lists of things to do, to get done. I have an organized mind. Last night when my husband didn't come home,

(The Girl mimes scrubbing pots downstage right in the vicinity of the tree)

I kept busy by scrubbing the pots. The pots need scrubbing because muck builds up in hard to reach places. If you let down your guard, even a little in the war against dirt, then you've lost, and dirt is everywhere, watching, waiting for an opportunity to pounce.

(Sudden realization as she wipes her hands on her apron)

My mother-in-law is coming for a visit. I have got to prepare myself. She doesn't know I am pregnant. I didn't want to have to tell her. I am afraid. Nothing I do is ever good enough for her.

(Trying to convince herself that she is happy)

I have everything I want. We have a car. And when he's home, my husband will drive me anywhere I want to go.

(Bends over to play with an imaginary dog)

We have a dog. Scamper. A loveable little mutt who shits in the house.

(Picking up an imaginary phone)

I wish the dog pound would come and take him away.

(Ghost enters and mimes doing her nails)

I've often picked up the phone and dialed them; the dog pound,

(Ghost mimes picking up the phone)

and when the woman with the grumpy voice says...

GHOST: Dog pound.

GIRL: I just sit there, breathing like an obscene caller. She says…

GHOST: Hello?… Hello?

(The Ghost hangs up the phone and exits the light)

GIRL: And then she hangs up. She hangs up because I say nothing, because the dog is sitting there, staring at me. The dog stares at me and I know what he's thinking. The dog is thinking that I want to get rid of him, and I don't like that. I don't like anyone, man or animal, thinking bad things about me, because I am very sweet, I practice being sweet. I practice being perfect.

When my husband courted me in the back seat of his chevy, he said to me that I was very…sweet.

I know I am in love because we have everything that a person could want.

(Ghost re-enters the light as Mrs. Harbour)

I know that the lady next door; Mrs. Harbour, who is all alone, she envies me.

(As if admiring herself in an imaginary mirror)

because I am young and pretty and have a handsome husband who cuts the grass, and builds bomb shelters, and takes out the garbage, before taking the dog, Scamper, for a walk.

(Ghost exits the light)

I never take Scamper for a walk. I am afraid he will break the leash, run off, and get hit by a vehicle, and even though I secretly want that to happen, I have learned to deny myself happiness.

I don't mean that. I mean my husband sacrifices for me and I sacrifice for my beautiful kitchen and living room.

(Mimes scrubbing pots)

My husband didn't come home last night, so I scrubbed the pots,

(Looks at the tree)

and when I heard the birds in the morning, at that time and place before the sky lightens, the birds making noise in that stupid tree that keeps me awake at night.

(As if in a nightmare)

Ghost of the Tree

I hear it scratching at the window like some lover,
like some twisted lover who wants to come in, who
wants to come in and wrap its barky arms around me
and pull me into the ground. And I swear I hear it
moaning in the night, a soul damned to hell.

(Turns brightly to the audience)

I thought of my lists.

Don't get me wrong. My husband is very romantic.
He calls me sugar and hon, and I call him…Danny.
He takes one and a half teaspoons of sugar in his
coffee and I tell him that he should cut down, that too
much sugar is not good for a person, because it rots
your teeth or gives you diabetes, or something. He
just looks at me like I have three heads. Is that what
people say when someone looks at them strange?

(Fearfully moving further downstage)

I have grown quite frightened. I am frightened of
several things. I hate looking at myself in the mirror. I
hate to see myself growing older, of dying, of melting
away. I hate the suspense of looking in the mirror and
anticipating what I will look like. On television
everyone is so happy.

And I am afraid of the dirt. Being afraid of dirt is my life.

(Getting very agitated)

I religiously clean, but nothing ever stays clean. It always gets dirty. And my hair. It never stays up. It always tickles my face and I try to get the wrinkles out of my clothes, but there are always more wrinkles…

(She has an epiphany)

That's why I don't like looking in the mirror. What if I become unattractive? What if I look like my mother? How can she be happy looking like she does? She's repulsive.

(Introspective)

I think I married too young.

(As if sharing a secret with the audience)

Sometimes I wish, and I know this is awful, but sometimes I wish that my husband would get in a car accident and become a quadriplegic, and then I could look after him, and I know he would never leave me, because I would have to feed him, and dress him, and make sure he could go to the bathroom. He could never leave me. He would become my prisoner, and then maybe, as he sat in his wheelchair, staring out the window, maybe I could get the courage to leave him, because I would think he was unattractive and see, who would want him then! But I don't think I could leave.

(Sits on the stool)

I don't think I could ever leave.

I wish the baby was dead.

(Stands up hopefully)

Is that him?

SCENE 5 The Lesbian Artist

Transition Scene.

Slow sensuous jazz music.

The Girl sits motionless on the stool.

There is an overhead light and leaf gobbo.

The Ghost removes the Girl's apron and returns it to the tree. She then brings the Girl a feather boa from the tree and drapes it around her shoulders. Then she brings the Girl a glass and a long cigarette holder from in front of the tree and hands it to the girl.

End of Transition.

Light changes to just an Amber Top Light.

GIRL: (*Holds drink in hand and mimes smoking with the cigarette holder*)

I smoke cigarettes, inhaling the hot embers, and churning out blue clouds of carbon monoxide, or dioxide, or maybe formaldehyde. Toxic clouds dulling the sun. I drink homemade gin.

(Expanded Amber pool of Light)

(Leaf gobbo)

Ghost of the Tree

GIRL: *(Mimes painting with the cigarette holder)*

And I paint, dripping oils on a thirsty canvas. There are so many ideas, intoxicating ideas, floating in the air, waiting to be grabbed. Recorded with a wet brush. I paint like...Pablo Picasso. I paint with liquids that dry into a fleeting image of life. The canvas; a slice of that life. A shaft of sunlight on pears and apples in a green ceramic bowl.

I paint the tree, the flowering oak, its darkness, its light, its paper thin leaves, its soul. I paint the soul that watches over me. Someday, I am sure, we will have to take it down. It was planted too near the house.

(The light brightens-Twenties dance music)

(The Ghost comes into the light and dances with the Girl)

I go to parties, parties all night long. And I talk to exciting people.

GHOST: *(Conspiratorially)*

They say your mother was the Queen of Egypt.

GIRL: I talk to communists, and unionists, and writers. I talk to criminals. Criminals haven't any ambiguity, any shades of gray. They rebel against the rule of law.

(Stops dancing and turns to talk to Ghost who mimes holding a drink in her hand)

My great grandmother; it was said, died in her bed of a shotgun blast. Her jealous husband found her in bed with another man; his business partner, and thus the family tree was poisoned by crime.

(To the audience)

Our parties go all night long. Debauchery and delirium.

(Music slows as Ghost touches her)

I have taken a lover. She is a writer, and we talk of the myriad possibilities.

(The Music stops)

(To the audience)

To be respectable, I have also married a man, a banker man. He says; Tom, my bankerman husband, says that numbers are language, simplified and beautified, that in conjunction with other numbers, create the world. One plus one equals three. That simple equation represents the human race.

(Admiring Ghost)

My writer friend is an intellectual, a, not to overuse the term; avant garde, She talks of women taking control of the world, taking control of their own lives. The future she says, will no longer be about men, but will be a shining bright light for women everywhere.

(Slow and sensual jazz music)

(The Girl flirts with the Ghost)

We talk of Eros, and the right of women to participate in the world, to work. To have the right to vote.

(The Girl turns away)

(The Music stops)

(The Ghost takes the Girl's hand and leads her to the stool)

But I have been dealt a tragic hand. I am pregnant, pregnant with a child, and I am depressed, depressed because a very bleak future has risen up out of the deep to confront me. I do not want this baby. Maybe I do. I don't know.

(The Ghost gently touches the Girl's belly)

But how can you lead the revolution and be fat with a human parasite eating away at your insides? My lover seems fascinated with my growing belly…

(The Girl stands up and moves downstage)

but I am not. I am afraid, afraid of being the baby's servant for the rest of my life. It is probably my husband's. Tom the banker man. I drink enough gin to kill a horse, but this thing growing inside of me will not die.

(The Girl mimes painting while the Ghost tries to touch her but the Girl becomes irritated, consumed with self-pity)

I paint myself growing all fat and absurd. I paint my rotting face, my elephantine skin.

GHOST: *(Exits after blowing a kiss to the Girl)*

GIRL: *(Looks unhappily at the disappearing Ghost)*

I paint the party disappearing in the distance, away from my chained body.

(To the audience)

Ghost of the Tree

Tom brought me flowers today. Wildflowers. Tom
the banker, too cheap to afford real flowers, real
store-bought flowers. He has to pick them from
someone's yard. Random genetic mutations.
Darwinian survival of the fittest. These particular
pretty little flowers, kicked the crap out of some other
pretty little flowers, in some mother earth cat fight.

(She looks up)

But what I want, what I yearn for, is the perfect music
of the spheres, the fact that man and in particular
woman, can breed life,

(Touching her belly)

shape it like genetic putty.

(Looks up)

I see the stars in the cold black sky and I want to
reach up, grab them and stick them in my eyes. I
dream of sucking on milky white stardust, of batting
bloated planets around the solar system. I dream of
watching life creating life, of inevitable decay, of
inevitable nothingness, which stretches like a ladder
into an impossible forever.

(To the audience)

I threw up today.

(The Girl sits back down on the stool)

(Lights fade to a spot on the stool)

I have been drinking way too much, or perhaps it is the baby. I feel very sick, poisoned by this life inside me. I don't know. I smoke and I drink.

Mathematics is simple and my husband says mathematics can explain everything, simply and beautifully. One plus one equals three. One man plus one woman equals a family of three, four, five, forever.

One plus one equals two. Me and my lover.

SCENE 6   The Brain-Damaged Girl

Transition Scene.

Distorted Music Box sound.

The Girl sits motionless on the stool.

There is an overhead light and leaf gobbo.

The Ghost takes the Girl's boa, glass and cigarette holder back to the tree. She then returns with a battered suitcase, with a red ribbon tied to the handle. She gives the suitcase to the Girl. The Ghost unties the girl's hair, letting it fall loose. She then retreats to the tree.

End of Transition.

Distorted Music Box sound ends.

Blue light and Leaf gobbo.

The following scene takes place outside at night.

GIRL: *(Sits on the stool awkwardly holding the suitcase on her lap-She laughs)*

Guess what? I ain't sposed to tell. I ain't sposed to tell no one. I git in trouble if I tell. Mama says I ain't sposed to tell. I ain't sposed to tell about it. Not to no one! I got sumthin' I gots a secret. I gots a real big secret! Mama says you gots to be quiet when you got a secret, an I gots one, a big one! Big, big secret!

Albert. You know Albert. He's a red haired. He's the helper. Always has the hammer and nails and makes all that noise. Bang! Bang! Bang!

(Laughs and then speaking softer)

Bang, bang, bang. All that noise. My mama, she gets these headaches from all his hammerin'. He's got to fix this and fix that.

Mama says my grampa got all crazy and took to drink, and let the place go. He caught my gramma in bed with a French guy and they wuz bare negged. They didn't have no clothes on and he wuz crazy mad and he shot them, Bang! Bang!

(Laughs)

Bang! Bang! Blew their heads off!

(Softer)

Blew their heads off.

(Stronger)

Upstairs, in the upstairs bedroom. Nobody ain't ever allowed up there. No! 'Cept, I went up there. I went up there with Albert. You know Albert. He's red-haired and freckles. Freckles come from the sun, he says. I ain't got no freckles, but…

(Laughs)

mebbe my baby might have freckles!

(Mortified)

Oh, I shouldn't have told. Mama's gonna give me hell now. Big hell for tellin' 'bout the secret. I ain't sposed to tell.

(Back to her version of normal)

'Cause Albert; Albert took me up to the room that nobody sposed to go in, that room that gramma got found all negged with the French man, the room that got locked up, but Albert, he took me up there, and he put me on the bed

(She doesn't really understand the significance of the next bit)

and he lied down on top of me. He lied down on top of me and now I gots this secret.

And mama and papa, they yell at each other all the time.

(Upset)

And Albert had to go away. They sent Albert away,

(Happy)

but Albert talked to me. Albert snuck up and talked to me. Albert said he would come for me at this night. He would come for me and we would be the king and queen of Egypt, like how I saw in the picture book, like the king and queen of Egypt.

(Distracted)

Then he lay on top of me again.

Mama and papa are sleepin', and I'm waitin' for Albert.

He was sposed to be here at midnight. I 'membered that, 'cause the big hand and the little hand are at the top. At the top was how Albert tol' me to remember the time. So I bin waitin' long time and it's gittin' cold, but I'm gonna stay here til Albert come for me and we kin be at Egypt. With all them snakes and...

Ghost of the Tree

(Trying to remember what is supposed to signify Egypt)

spears and stuff.

(Laughs)

When I was little, my mama said that I played in the tree, that I climbed high in the tree. Mama said I was a little monkey. Where is she? They'd all say. Where's that girl gone to? And papa or mama would say; dumb girl she's up in the tree again!

Mama said that I was the smartest prettiest girl in the whole wide world. Mama said, an' she said I used to dance. Dance like I was floatin', floatin' on 'a air…

(Whispers)

Air…

(Upset)

I can't remember that. I can't remember dancing. I don't know how, I don't know how to dance.

(Proudly)

The smartest prettiest girl in the whole world, and papa said I was Queen of Egypt...Queen of Egypt.

Charles Robertson

(Frustrated)

But everythin' from before, everythin' is all dark, like the sky now. Everythin' is hard to remember.

(Looks up at the tree with wonder)

I climbed up one day. Climbed up real high.

(Sound of distorted music box)

I remember someone fallin', fallin' through the branches. I remember a scream like a bird or sumthin', sumthin' screamin' in my ears. And a little girl going over and over like a leaf, like a leaf fallin'. I remember the little girl fallin'.

(Music Box sound stops)

Mama says it was me, but I don't remember that. It was somebody else, another girl, a pretty girl that could dance and sing and that was the prettiest, smartest girl in the whole world.

(Matter of factly)

I don't climb that tree no more.

It's gittin' cold. Hope Albert comes soon.

(Happy again)

You remember Albert. He's a red-haired an freckles. I got a lil baby doll inside a me. A little princess. And Albert n me-

(Upset)

I wanna keep the baby, cause Mama said I ain't smart enough no more to take care of a kid and they were gonna call the police on Albert so he gots to sneak back to get me.

(Uncomfortable)

But its gittin' cold. Hope he comes soon.

(Like the Little Match Girl being warmed by her imagination, the images of the picture book warms the Girl)

I just keep thinkin' of that picture book of Egypt. And its so hot and warm there- And the crocodiles. But the crocodiles only eat the poor folk and not the queens. Nuthin' happens to the queens, specially in Egypt.

(Suddenly has a sad memory)

I just remembered sumthin'. I just remembered sumthin' about the lil girl that fell from that tree. I remember seein' her fall. I hope she's alright. I hope she didn't get hurt too bad. She was pretty. She was a pretty girl.

(Suddenly abandoning her idea of running away with Albert)

I should go inside now. Mama and Papa will be mad. I should go inside now.

SCENE 7 The English Bride

Transition Scene.

Music suggesting England from the eighteen hundreds.

The Girl sits motionless on the stool.

There is an overhead light and leaf gobbo.

The Ghost takes away the battered suitcase and returns it to the tree. She returns with a red nineteenth century hat. She puts up the Girl's hair and attaches the hat with bobby pins if need be.

End of Transition.

Bright pool of light.

The following scene suggests day time. The tree has not been planted yet, so no gobbo is needed.

GHOST: (*Takes the Girl's hand and leads the Girl downstage*)

Your husband advertised for a wife in the London papers and as you had education, much education, but no money, your family having consumed itself financially, driven mad by misfortune and sexual excess, you answered the ad.

(Ghost exits the light)

(The Music stops)

GIRL: My husband is a sweating pig. I don't much like him but I must be resolute. I have undertaken this marriage, this partnership and perhaps in time we can learn to become amiable. This country however is not amiable. It is unfriendly, uncivilized. The streets are dirt. There are some buildings of note.

(Looks up)

This house my husband is building for me is quite nice, quite large, so that I can escape to the far reaches and hide. It is four stories high, and they have dragged stone blocks from the surrounding mines to build it. My husband, my architect has decided to name the house in my honour.

(To the audience)

I suppose I should be flattered. I am not however privy to feelings of unmixed delight. He calls it The England House because…I am from England. The man has no poetry.

Ghost of the Tree

(She mimes painting)

Painting I have taken up. I look out my window and I
paint the waves, imagining the ocean, imagining
England. I came from the ocean, fully formed. A
Hans Christian Anderson mermaid.

(Clutches her arms as if suddenly cold)

And like his mermaid I have turned to stone.

(To the audience)

What greeted me upon my arrival was the shabbiest
collection of architecture by convenience. The trees
run riot in this miserable land, and

(Looks up)

there are so many birds in the sky, it turns black with
feathers and rains white runny shit. I wish someone
would shoot them all.

(To the audience)

My husband sent me no picture but I half expected,
half-hoped, but I am sure he must be the ugliest man
in this god-forsaken land, and that is saying quite a
lot. Gerald his name is, my husband, I mean. He has
entered into partnership with another fellow.

(She brightens)

Henri. As can be supposed from his name, he is French, very romantic, not to be trusted around the ladies, which makes him ever so much more appealing.

(Back to previous state)

The partnership has been entered into with the promise, the hope of making beer.

Apparently there is a great appetite for beer in this wilderness. From what I have witnessed beer drives men mad, and leads to belching, belching and the creation of babies. People want to get drunk to forget, apparently to forget that they are in this godforsaken land.

A couple of hungry Indian children showed up in town the other day. I was quite frightened. I had never seen one before, which is odd, because the country was over run, if that is perhaps the word I might wish to use, but the British government has done a marvellous job of keeping them out of sight. They must learn to join proper society or they will disappear.

And the stores. I can't quite come up with words to describe the paucity of the stores. Wooden frame stores that sells last years hats. I dread anyone from England visiting and seeing me dressed like some street peddler, garbed in clothes that have been tossed in the trash by the best society.

I have tried beer. I do not like it. It makes me rather loud, which I do not care for. After consuming a quantity of beer, my husband paws at me and tries to entice me into the bedroom, which I have been quite adept at avoiding. I am pregnant, so I suppose I will have to lie down with him at some point.

(Touches her belly)

This creature growing in my belly was a present from my husband's business partner.

(To audience)

We meet secretly. He is French Canadian but I don't hold it against him.

My husband took me to the brewery the other day, to show me the machines for making beer.

(Touching an imaginary Henri)

At a discreet moment I went up to Henri to touch him, to hold him. I cannot live without him. I am trapped by my feelings for him, but he pushes me away.

(Steps back)

He said we shouldn't be seen together, that I was being indiscreet, that Gerald would surely find out. So, what? I replied, laughing at him. Silly boy, what was Gerald going to do if he did find out? Shoot us? We live, I reminded poor frightened Henri, we live in a civilized society, in an age of ideals. People just don't go round killing each other for love.

(Moves to the tree without stepping out of the centre light)

(Music begins again)

I planted a tree in his honour, in Henri's honour. I call it…the French tree. My own shocking little secret. A wild thing planted near the brick and mortar of our, oh so ordinary marriage.

The French tree.

I wonder if it will outlast me.

SCENE 8 The Final Scene

Transition.

Melancholic Music.

The Girl sits motionless on the stool.

There is an overhead light and leaf gobbo.

The Ghost takes the hat from the Girl and returns it to the tree. The Ghost then grabs the red coat from the tree and puts it on the Girl. The Ghost puts the Girl's hair down so it is hanging loose. The Ghost then retreats to the tree.

End of Transition.

Leaf gobbo and dim light.

GIRL: (*Stands up and approaches the audience*)

You see; what I'm gonna do is straighten out my life. I'm gonna make it. You see, Johnny; he's good with kids. People don't understand him. They don't see what I see, what's underneath. Every couple has their problems.

That night he went crazy. I started it. It wasn't his fault. It's just that he loves me so much. I never had anyone love me like that.

I got this idea that me n' Johnny and the baby, we could live here. Fix the place up. This could be the baby's room. Decorate it real nice, and I would love my baby. 'Cause babies, they need love, so we gotta help them out. And I won't hurt my baby, or leave it on some doorstep.

(Music might fade out here)

I wish Johnny was here right now. I need someone to hold onto. I gotta get Johnny a suit for the wedding. I thought we'd have this big garden party wedding under the tree.

(The Ghost enters the light and the Girl freezes in fear when she sees the Ghost. The Ghost sits down on the floor behind the Girl)

GIRL; (*Moves downstage to get away from the Ghost*)

Oh, yeah, uh, I dunno. I don't feel so good. Invite all our friends, even Crazy Hank. I know champagne's expensive, but...Oh!

Ghost of the Tree
(She suffers from a debilitating wave of Pain)

Where is he? He said he would be here. Johnny could get a job in construction, and I could do movies and our little girl, I know it's going to be a girl. She'll be loved so much.

(Another wave of Pain)

Did I tell you I used to wanted to be an actress? My mom put me in lessons. That's when she still gave a shit. Me and her, we used to watch these movies and we used to dream that I would be up there in that perfect world.

(Looks at the tree)

Look at that. The family tree; its coming down.

(Lights out on tree)

(Melancholic music starts up again)

(The Girl starts to give in to her tears)

When I was high I had this dream, a warm sunshine dream of a little girl picking flowers.

And the tree is big, with many branches, and cool green leaves. And the tree, old and big as it is, seems as if it will go on forever. And the leaves in the wind, I realize it is only a tree, only a life, and the winters, and the wind, broken down by disease, the tree will come down, like all trees.

(The Girl turns and approaches the Ghost. The Girl is having trouble walking-she is very upset)

Mom? Something's wrong. I tried to….

GHOST: Shh… eventually, the wooden corpse will be eaten away,

(Reaches her hand up to the Girl)

and the hungry meadow will reach up

(The Girl takes the Ghost's hand)

and pull it into the ground.

(The Girl curls up on the Ghost's lap)

And there will be nothing

(The Girl struggles up but the Ghost gently stops her)

Shh…Nothing but the wind in the grass.

(Looks at the tree)

Such is the fate of trees.

(Looks at the audience)

And the little girl and the mom will be gone.

(Lights out quickly)

FINI.

Charles Robertson
ABOUT THE AUTHOR

Charles Robertson is a playwright and director in Canada
who has been involved in all facets of theatre.
He has written a number of plays for young people,
including *Pretty Pieces* and *Til the Boys Come Home*
With partner Anne Marie Mortensen, he runs
Bottle Tree Productions at www.bottletreeinc.com
Bottle Tree Productions offers free acting advice and
monologues for aspiring actors.
Bottle Tree Productions One Act Play Competition for
Writers has a One Thousand Dollar First Prize and closes on
November 30th of each year.